Shop for C

CU00922076

A Comedy

Charles Mander

Samuel French – London
New York – Sydney – Toronto – Hollywood

CHARACTERS

Hilda
Doris
Brenda
Mrs Pike
Mr Galbraith

The action of the play takes place in a small shop selling second-hand goods for charity in almost any town

Time — the present

SHOP FOR CHARITY

A small charity shop, in almost any town. A Friday afternoon in Spring

The shop sells second-hand garments and a wide selection of cast-off knick-knacks for charity. It is a musty, makeshift little place as though thrown together in a hurry. UR, *set at an angle, is a trestle table covered with a chenille cloth, which serves as a counter. On it is a fairly sophisticated, extremely incongruous and barely functional electronic till. Odd bits and pieces adorn the counter. Behind it are a number of shelves littered with old toys and games etc. Two bentwood chairs squat uneasily at each end of the counter amongst a clutter of old tennis raquets, croquet mallets and an umbrella.* DR *and* DL *stand numerous racks or tables containing a motley selection of second-hand garments – petticoats, underclothes, coats and so on – in no particular order. There are one or two large cardboard boxes brimming over with unpacked old clothes. The whole place is something of a muddle.* UL, *at an angle, is a window with a cardboard notice saying:* CLOSED *on the side facing the audience, and* OPEN *on the other side. At an angle to this is an archway* L, *leading to the shop entrance. A similar archway* DR *leads to the staff entrance. This archway is hung with beads and has a notice saying:* PRIVATE. STAFF ONLY

When the CURTAIN *rises the stage is empty. We hear distant traffic noises. A pale shaft of spring sunlight fights its way through the dusty window. A bell tinkles and the shop door slams*

Hilda, the shop manageress, enters L, *carrying a plastic bag. She is a formidable, middle-aged lady with a North-Country accent. She casts a beady eye about her domain*

Hilda (*commandingly*) Shop!

There is no discernible reply

I said shop!

*An intense shriek rends the air from the direction of the "Staff Only"
archway* DR. *The shriek comes from Brenda, who is in the toilet. Hilda
shows some distaste but no particular surprise .*

Brenda (*off, hysterically*) Get away! Get away! This is for ladies
  only!
Hilda (*irritably*) Oh, not again! (*Going* R *and calling*) Brenda?
Brenda?
Brenda (*off, hysterically*) You can't come in here. It's engaged.

  Doris enters DR. *She is a small, bustling woman. She carries a cup
  and saucer*

Hilda I know, don't tell me. You don't have to tell me.
Doris (*going to the counter and placing the cup and saucer on it*) I
  tried to lure her out, but I think she's beyond it.
Brenda (*off*) Help! Help! Send for the police!
Hilda Stupid woman! She'll have to go. She's turning the shop into
  a madhouse.
Doris (*fiddling with the till*) I wish you would explain this
  appliance, Hilda. I cannot get it to function. Whenever I try to
  get it open it tells me the time.
Hilda Drunk as a sailor, I suppose.
Doris There, you see. Look, it's telling me the time. I don't want to be
  told the time. Why does everything have to be so complicated
  these days? I suppose modern technology has left me behind.
  Would you like a cup of tea, dear? There's plenty in the pot.
Brenda (*off*) Go away! Go away, filthy beast!
Doris Mr Galbraith was in this morning. I think he upset her. I'm
  glad you turned up, Hilda, I was beginning to despair.
Hilda She'll have to go. I'll have to speak to the area manager.
Doris Oh no! I mean Brenda's been here for years. She was one of
  our first helpers, and it's part of her life, Hilda. It keeps her going.
Hilda She's a damned nuisance, Doris, and you know it. All that
  caterwauling and sitting in the toilet — it puts the customers off.
  She'll have to go.
Doris But this is a charity shop, Hilda.
Hilda What's that got to do with it?
Doris I put it down to Mr Galbraith. You know what he's like.
Hilda (*looking disgusted*) Only too well! But there is little we can do
  about Mr Galbraith, apart from summoning the police, and
  they're reluctant. She's gone very quiet.

Doris I expect she's dropped off, she usually does. I think she finds it exhausting. Do let me get you a cup of tea.

Hilda No, thank you. I suppose we've not had any customers?

Doris Oh yes, one or two. We've had one or two, and Mr Galbraith. Old Mrs Pike is upstairs.

Hilda What's she doing here? It's not her day.

Doris Pricing, I think.

Hilda Pricing? She's no business to be pricing. That's my job. I do the pricing. Who told her she could do the pricing?

Doris Nobody I suppose. You know what she's like. Switches off her hearing aid and nobody can get through.

Hilda (*snorting*) Pricing indeed. What does she know about pricing? That woman is not even metricated. I'll have to stop it at once. (*She marches to the entrance* DR)

Brenda totters in DR. *She is a colourful, rather extravagant-looking woman in her sixties. She had, in earlier years, been attractive and lively but is now gone to seed*

Brenda (*to Hilda*) Did you see him?

Hilda Who?

Brenda The man! He leaped at me from behind the lingerie. God, it was horrible.

Hilda I wish you would try and pull yourself together, Brenda.

Brenda totters towards Doris and ignores Hilda

Brenda He was like a wild beast. I could feel his hot breath on my neck. I am always being set upon by men, Doris. It's so unfair.

Hilda (*impatiently*) Stuff and nonsense!

Brenda (*emotionally*) What do you know about it, Hilda? I doubt if you have ever been bothered.

Doris (*soothingly*) There, there. It's all over. Sit down, Brenda. I made you a cup of tea.

She offers Brenda a chair

Brenda (*sagging into the chair*) Oh, you're so good to me, Doris. So understanding. (*Scowling at Hilda*) A light shining in the wilderness. Has anybody seen my shopping bag? I left it somewhere. (*She peers about half-heartedly*)

Doris takes the cup and saucer from the counter and trots off DR

Hilda We all know what it contains.
Brenda It's so unfair. It's so damned unfair. They have lusting eyes, you know, and their hands sweat.
Hilda Oh really!
Brenda He came out of the lingerie like a mad bull, snorting and pawing the ground.
Hilda I think it is about time that we had a serious conversation, Brenda. This cannot go on, and if you will not give up the you-know-what, then you must give up the shop.
Brenda (*throwing up her hands and bursting into tears*) Yes, yes. Cast me aside, fling me into the wilderness. Oh, it's so unfair, so unfair. (*She buries her head in her hands and rocks back and forth in the chair*)

Doris enters DR *carrying a cup of tea*

Doris Oh, heavens. (*To Hilda*) You've set her off again, Hilda.
Hilda I'm trying to run a charity shop, not a madhouse. I have to think of the customers.
Doris Come along, Brenda. You'll feel better when you've had this.

Doris gives Brenda the cup

Brenda It's so unfair. Nobody believes me. Nobody has ever believed me. But it happens, you see. It happens.

She is about to drink the tea when the sound of shuffling steps can be heard quite loudly, descending the stairs off, behind the staff entrance DR

Oh, my God. What's that?

She goes rigid, and in spite of themselves both Doris and Hilda for a moment catch her alarm. The steps approach

Mrs Pike shuffles in DR. *She is a small, frail, elderly lady. Although she is very deaf, she has remarkable energy for her age. She is carrying a pair of gent's long combinations, held out before her like an offering*

Mrs Pike How much does one put on these do you think? My husband used to get them from Wellworthy's for twelve and six a pair, but I suppose that would be too much to ask. (*Looking accusingly at Hilda*) Somebody has been in the toilet for nearly half an hour.

Hilda You shouldn't be here, Mrs Pike.

Mrs Pike It's a good job I wasn't taken short.

Hilda (*bellowing*) You shouldn't be here. It's not your day.

Mrs Pike What?

Brenda Lust and violence. (*Scowling at Hilda*) And compassion has flown out of the window!

Hilda (*at the end of her tether*) That is enough. That is quite enough. It is high time, Brenda, that you took your problems elsewhere. And as for you, Mrs Pike, you have no business to be here on a Friday afternoon. (*She snatches the combinations from Mrs Pike*) I'll take those, if you don't mind. I am in charge of pricing, not you. I would remind you ladies that the purpose of this establishment is to sell second-hand goods to provide funds for supplying food and useful implements to the under-nourished nations of the Third World. We are here to serve that purpose, not to sit about drinking cups of tea and locking ourselves in the toilet.

Hilda sweeps majestically DS *and goes to sieze an article from a hanger, when she finds it isn't there. She glares round accusingly*

Where is it?

Doris What?

Hilda The red velvet coat and skirt. I left it here. Where is it?

Doris Oh. Did it have black buttonholes?

Hilda Yes.

Doris And black trimming round the collar?

Hilda It did.

Doris I sold it.

Hilda You what?

Doris I sold it. The lady seemed to take a fancy to it, so I sold——

Hilda (*bitterly*) Oh thank you. Thank you very much. That is my daughter's coat and skirt. I have just had it cleaned!

Doris Oh dear. I'm sorry, Hilda but it was on the hanger and it seemed to have a price tag on it.

Hilda That was the cleaner's tag. One of these days I shall do something violent, I swear. I shall do something violent.

She glares about her malevolently than stalks out DR

There is a pregnant silence

Mrs Pike My grandfather went funny towards the end of his life.

He believed he could control the weather. Of course, it didn't rain so much in those days. I can't think why Hilda wants those combinations, they're far too big for her.

Mrs Pike trots out DR

Doris Oh dear. Poor Hilda. I suppose I should have looked. Perhaps the lady will come back. Oh dear.
Brenda (*giggling*) Serves her right. She gets more out of this shop than the Third World as it is. We ought to stand up to her.
Doris That's unkind, Brenda. Hilda is dedicated. (*Going behind the counter*) I wish I could open this till. I feel so helpless in the face of technology. (*To Brenda*) Feeling better?
Brenda You don't believe what I say, do you?
Doris Do you expect me to believe it?
Brenda No. People have never believed me, even when it has been the truth.
Doris It's easier not to believe. It's easier not to believe in all sorts of things.
Brenda I know. I found that out once. When I was a little girl.
Doris (*going to the window*) I think if we were situated closer to the High Street we might do better business.
Brenda They wouldn't believe it. Didn't want to believe it. Too embarrassing, you see. His breath smelt of salami and stale beer and his neck was dirty.
Doris Mrs Pike must be rising eighty, but she is full of energy. It's quite amazing.
Brenda "Come here, little girl. Do you fancy a whipped cream walnut?" They were very popular in those days, and very tasty. Greed, that's what it was, just greed. Adam fell for the apple and I fell for a whipped cream walnut. They didn't believe me, and I had run all the way home, and I was crying, but they didn't believe me. They sent me to bed. They sent me to bed for telling lies. And I've told lies ever since.
Doris (*going to one of the boxes and producing a garment*) I think we should put these garments on to hangers. They've been priced.
Brenda I embarrass you. I embarrass everybody. I've no business here. (*Starting to weep*) Oh, God, I'm useless. I'm bloody useless.
Doris Oh nonsense, Brenda. You're good company. The only thing is——
Brenda I drink.

Doris Couldn't you get dried out? I mean, lots of people do. My husband did.

Brenda From the troubles of this world I turn to gin.

Doris Ducks.

Brenda What?

Doris I think it was ducks that he turned to.

Brenda What use are ducks? Ducks can't help you forget, can't ease the burden. I wish I knew where I had left that shopping bag. I need something stronger than tea, I really do.

Hilda marches in DR

Hilda Somebody has vomited in the toilet. Who ever did it should clean it up.

Doris I'll see to it. (*She starts to go*)

Brenda (*with dignity*) No! I will see to it.

Brenda exits DR, *her head high*

Hilda She'll have to go. It's all over the floor. Revolting.

Doris (*returning to her chores at the box*) Brenda is not well.

Hilda She's a damned sight too fond of the bottle.

Doris She is not well.

Hilda Then what is she doing here?

Doris What are any of us doing here?

Hilda begins to speak

Brenda is no more broken than the rest of us. She's more obvious, that's all.

Hilda Well that's a funny way of looking at it, I must say. A very odd way.

Doris (*holding up a dress*) I wonder if this would go with my blue hat. (*She takes it across to the window to get the daylight*) I'm fond of Brenda. I wouldn't want to stay here without her.

Hilda And what do you mean by that, may I ask?

Doris I think I'll put this aside. It's quite nice. (*She folds the dress and places it in her shopping bag behind the counter*)

Hilda Oh it's easy for you. You just come here once a week. You don't have the responsibility. You don't have the burden of keeping this place running on the right lines. We're here to help the starving, you know. Not Brenda.

Doris (*sighing*) I suppose you're right. (*Smiling distantly*) You generally are.

Hilda Of course I'm right. You know damned well I'm right. They — (*sweeping her arm in the general direction of the window*) — they need the help, the starving masses of upper India and such places. The subcontinents. They need the help, and I like to think that we in this shop are doing our little bit. Making our little sacrifices for — them. (*Once more sweeping her arm round towards the window*) Oh heck!

Galbraith appears at the window. He is a scruffy, hairy tramp-like person in a raincoat. He is in his fifties. You can almost smell him through the window. He is grinning and gesticulating

Hilda stalks to the window and waves her arms as though driving cattle out of a garden

Go away. Go away. You're not wanted here!

The apparition smiles and waves back

Hop it. Go on, hop it! (*She gesticulates furiously*)

Galbraith holds up a large notice and points to it, grinning. The notice says: MOAB SHALL HOWL OVER NEBO

Doris It's Mr Galbraith. I expect he wants a cup of tea and a biscuit. He said he'd be back.

Hilda I won't have that dirty old man in my shop. Go away, do you hear?

Galbraith grins, waves and disappears

If he comes in here I shall call the police.

The shop door tinkles and a moment later Galbraith is framed in the archway L

Hilda glowers at him

Galbraith (*enthusiastically*) Ha! (*To Hilda*) I see before me a woman of stature. Comely as Jerusalem, terrible as an army with banners. Give us a kiss, love.

Hilda (*backing away*) Don't you dare! (*Wagging a finger at him*) You come near me and I'll clock you one!

Galbraith Stay me with flagons. Comfort me with apples, for I am sick with love.

He prances towards Hilda

Hilda (*retreating*) Get away. You're disgusting!

Doris Now don't be naughty, Mr Galbraith.

Galbraith Draw me, I will run after thee. The queen hath brought me into her chambers.

Hilda flaps at him and beats a retreat DR

Hilda Get off! Go away. You're not wanted here. Get rid of him, Doris. He's a proper pest.

Galbraith prances and sways about

Galbraith He cometh leaping upon the mountains, skipping upon the hills.

Hilda begins to retreat through the staff entrance DR

Hilda For heaven's sake! And you can't come in here. It's for staff only.

Hilda exits DR

Doris I told you not to be naughty, Mr Galbraith. Hilda is quite capable of calling the police. Now sit down and behave yourself. (*She points to a chair*)

Galbraith (*collapsing on to the chair and breathing heavily from his efforts*) By Jove, a veritable woman; makes the blood surge. I could do with a cup of tea.

Doris Not unless you behave yourself. And you shouldn't keep coming in here for cups of tea. We're not a charity.

Galbraith turns and catches her eye

Well, not that sort of charity. Oh very well. I shall get you a cup of tea if you promise not to steal any garments whilst I am away.

Gabraith (*with dignity*) Here sits a man of honour, madam. Upright and godly. I am no nicker of garments. Perish the thought.

Doris Well, behave yourself.

Doris trots out DR

Once Doris has gone Galbraith makes for the till and presses a key speculatively. It pings startlingly and Galbraith springs back

Galbraith Great God! (*The machine pings, clicks and finally zips. He peers at it as though it might bite him, and then dismisses it with* *a disdainful shrug. He leans over the counter and comes up with Brenda's bag)* Hullo, what have we here? (*He delves into the bag and produces a half bottle of gin)* Mother's ruin. Strong drink shall be bitter to them that drink it. Another good lady fallen, I fear. (*He undoes the bottle and takes a long swig)*

Mrs Pike ambles in DR

Mrs Pike I really do not believe that a second-hand pair of gent's long combinations will reach more than five shillings.

Galbraith, caught in full swig, splutters and hurriedly returns the bottle to its bag and clutches his heart

There cannot be much of a market for second-hand reach-me-downs, and yet she insists on ten shillings.

Galbraith Monstrous, madam. Monstrous.

Mrs Pike Oh. It's you, Mr Galbraith, I hope you haven't been at the till again.

Galbraith That is a calumny, madam.

Mrs Pike What?

Galbraith A cal—— (*giving up*) oh, never mind.

Mrs Pike (*suspiciously*) You look furtive, Mr Galbraith.

Galbraith It is my natural manner. I cannot help it. Some people look upright and honest, others furtive. It's the way of things.

Mrs Pike (*severely*) You would look less furtive if you were not clutching Brenda's bag.

Galbraith What? Oh.

He puts the bag to one side. Mrs Pike starts to put her coat on

Going?

Mrs Pike Pardon?

Galbraith grimaces and says nothing

Doris enters with a cup of tea

Doris You really must not make a habit of expecting cups of tea whenever you come here, Mr Galbraith. Now drink this up and vamoose. (*To Mrs Pike*) You're not going?

Galbraith She is disconnected.

Doris (*bellowing*) You're not going, Mrs Pike?

Mrs Pike Yes, dear, yes. I know when I am not wanted. And when you reach my age you are seldom wanted.

Galbraith Nor I, madam, nor I. Cheers. (*He raises his cup in a toast*)
Doris What nonsense.
Mrs Pike I do not see how you can expect anybody to pay ten
    shillings for a second-hand pair of gent's combinations.

Mrs Pike exits L. *The doorbell tinkles*

Doris Oh dear. Poor Mrs Pike. (*Brooding for a moment*) Do hurry
    up, Mr Galbraith. If Hilda returns . . . .
Galbraith And in that day seven women shall take hold of one
    man. Now that's a sobering thought, madam. A sobering
    thought.
Doris What are you talking about?
Galbraith I am contemplating the prophets. Profoundly.
Doris You have been drinking.
Galbraith I am familiar with the bible. There was little else to read
    in my last habitation. Little else.

*Doris moves over to a box and starts sorting out the garments.
Galbraith quickly conveys the gin bottle from the bag to his pocket,
and continues gloomily sipping his tea*

Brenda enters DR

    (*Brightening at the sight of Brenda*) Ha! Three score queens, four
    score concubines and virgins without number.
Brenda (*throbbing dramatically*) How dare you! How dare you!
Doris (*warningly*) Brenda! Not again, please. Come and help me
    sort out these garments.

*Brenda teeters on the edge of another frenzy but thinks better of it.
She glares ferociously at Galbraith, then joins Doris*

Brenda (*whispering loudly and elaborately*) That man interferes
    with me.
Doris (*holding up a pair of gent's patent leather shoes*) I wonder
    what size these are? (*She turns them over looking for the size*)
Brenda That man is a sexual deviant. Doris, I need a drink. Have
    you seen my bag?

Galbraith refreshes himself surreptitiously from the bottle of gin

Galbraith The daughters of Zion are haughty, and walk with
    stretched forth necks and wanton eyes. (*He belches*) Pardon.

Brenda (*preparing to be dramatic and screwing up her eyes*) Ahh!
Doris That is quite enough, Mr Galbraith. You have had your tea
  and you must go.
Galbraith How is thy faithful city become an harlot!
Doris (*going to Galbraith*) Fiddlesticks. Now run along. (*She picks
  up the cup of tea and starts going towards the staff entrance*)
Galbraith Everyone loveth gifts and followeth after rewards. They
  judge not the fatherless.

Doris exits DR

*Galbraith, now fairly carried away, produces the gin bottle and swigs
it again*

Everyone is an hypocrite and an evil doer and every mouth
speaketh folly.
Brenda (*suspecting*) My God!

Brenda goes over to Galbraith, discovers her bag and scrabbles in it

(*Furiously*) You drunken swine! Give it here! (*She makes a grab
at the bottle, rattling Galbraith's teeth in the process*)

Galbraith (*spluttering*) Avaunt, frenzied woman!

He makes off, pursued by Brenda

The Lord will smite with a scab the crown of thy head.
Brenda Give it back. It's mine. Mine. (*She makes a dart at him*)
Galbraith The rings and nose jewels.

Brenda lunges at him and he flaps away

The changeable suits of apparel.

Brenda has another go

The mantles and the wimples and the crisping pins.

Brenda beats him over the head with her bag

Hell's bells, madam, lay off. (*Thrusting the bottle at her*) Take the
bloody thing and be damned.

Brenda swigs the remains of the gin

Brenda Exeter or Wandsworth?
Galbraith Pardon?

Brenda You didn't learn all that twaddle in a seminary, Galbraith, that I'll swear.

Galbraith Do I see before me a fellow outcast? Another pimple on the backside of governance?

Brenda swigs again

Brenda My God, I needed that. You swine, Galbraith. This is my life's blood, and you would filch it. Jesus, how I hate men.

Galbraith (*thoughtfully*) Children are their oppressors and women rule over them.

Brenda That will be the day. (*She grins wryly*)

Galbraith It is the day. For they have rewarded evil unto themselves. And they have not exalted the humble and meek. So children are their oppressors and women rule over them. Do you know how to work this till?

Brenda No.

Galbraith Pity.

Brenda That's a dark deed in a dirty world; rifling the till of a charity shop. How like a man.

Galbraith I was thinking of your life's blood—(*nodding at the nearly empty gin bottle*) – and my own desperate plight. Charity begins at home.

Brenda Perfidious bastard! (*She takes another swig*)

Galbraith I exist, therefore I am.

Brenda Swine.

Galbraith Do they exist, I ask myself. These shadows that so obsess the good ladies of this emporium.

Brenda Ravishing young girls with whipped cream walnuts. Tearing at their knickers. (*She takes another swig*)

Galbraith Do they exist? Do they wither on the doorstep? Charity begins at home. Open the till, madam. In God's name.

Brenda (*throwing away the bottle dramatically*) Take me!

Galbraith What?

Brenda Take me. Sieze me with your gnarled hands. I am but a weak defenceless woman. (*Flinging out her arms*) I submit!

Galbraith Now look here, madam.

Brenda I know what you have in mind! Lust, lust, lust.

Galbraith First things first; open the till.

Brenda Never! Never! Take me! Ravish me. I cannot stop you.

Galbraith I do not want to take you, madam. I am not that way inclined.

Brenda You swine! You perverted swine. It's boys you're after, is it?

Galbraith Certainly not. Kindly keep your voice down.

Brenda Disgusting monster! You're all the same. Aah! (*She rushes dramatically towards the staff entrance*)

Doris enters DR

Doris Brenda! Oh heck!

Brenda Get away ... get away!

Brenda sweeps Doris aside as she hurries out DR

We hear a door slam. The till, suddenly reacting to Galbraith's furtive efforts to open it, goes into a frenzy of pings, zips and flashing lights. Galbraith quickly tries to disguise it with his raincoat

Hilda (*distantly; off*) What on earth is going on down there? Doris ... Doris.

Doris (*calling back*) It's all right, Hilda. Just a spot of bother with the till.

Hilda Well, it sounds like an orgy.

Doris (*to Galbraith*) Well?

Galbraith That woman is a victim of delirium tremens, madam. I swear I've never been so beset by such a maddened harridan.

Doris Never mind that. Why were you trying to rob the till?

Galbraith Till? What till?

Doris I suppose you realize that the little we collect here goes to people who are literally starving.

Galbraith A pious thought, madam. To buy salvation for the price of a pair of second-hand gentleman's long combinations. Er, with respect.

Doris You are a thief, Mr Galbraith and a humbug, and I think you had better go before I call the police.

Galbraith That, madam, would be charity indeed.

Doris And what exactly do you mean by that?

Galbraith Three months or so in the custody of Her Britannic Majesty would see me through the worst of the winter and enable me to continue with my theological expositions beyond the prophet Isaiah. Call the police, madam. Do me a favour. A place of refuge for a shadow in the daytime, and a covert from storm and from rain. Chapter four, verse six. More or less. (*He sits*)

Doris Oh don't be so silly. You are not without means. You are good for nothing, Mr Galbraith and I suspect it is from choice and not necessity.

Galbraith They have eyes and see not!

Doris I am not blind.

Galbraith Oh yes you are, madam. With respect. You are all blind, all you good women.

Doris You must go, and there's an end to it.

Galbraith Make the heart of this people fat.

Doris We cannot have you continually in here.

Galbraith Make their ears heavy and shut their eyes.

Doris Smelling like an open drain.

Galbraith Lest they see with their eyes——

Doris Stealing the stock and——

Galbraith —and hear with their ears, and understand with their heart.

Doris —upsetting Brenda and driving away the customers. You are more than we can bear, Mr Galbraith. You are not to be tolerated. So please leave us alone.

Galbraith Yes! That is what they all say. Please leave us alone. Leave us alone. Leave us alone. (*He flaps and gibbers*)

Doris Stop it. Stop it!

Galbraith (*imitating her*) Stop it. Stop it!

Doris (*distraught*) Please, Mr Galbraith. Please.

Galbraith (*his eyes are cunning and cruel*) The daughters of Zion are haughty and walk with stretched forth necks.

Galbraith moves closer to Doris

Doris Please, please.

Galbraith Therefore the Lord will smite with a scab the crown of the head of the daughters of Zion. (*Moving closer; whispering*) And the Lord will discover their secret parts. And in that day the Lord will take away the bravery of their tinkling ornaments.

Doris You're mad and you're drunk. Please leave me alone.

Galbraith (*relaxing the tension a little*) There you go again. "Please leave me alone." But it won't do, madam, it won't do. I exist, and I am. And you cannot make me go away by closing your eyes and selling second-hand clothes for the benefit of the Third World.

Because that is what you are trying to do, is it not? You and the good ladies.

Doris No. No.

Galbraith Oh yes I think it is. A little light task of a voluntary nature for the doubtful benefit of distant humanity, helps to soothe the small prickings of conscience, wouldn't you say?

Doris At least I have a conscience, Mr Galbraith. I wonder if you do.

Galbraith I don't need a conscience, madam. I am a vagrant. My soul is already lost. I don't need a conscience.

Doris (*disturbed*) It is the best I can do. I am not rich. I have no influence, no power. It's the best I can do. Now look. (*Delving into her purse*) If you are really short——

Galbraith (*leaping up and brandishing his arms*) Bribery! Thy silver has become dross.

Doris What do you want? Just exactly what do you want? Please tell me.

Galbraith A vineyard like Solomon, a fountain of gardens, a well of living waters and streams from Lebanon.

Doris (*doubtfully*) I don't think I could go as far as——

Galbraith A fiver would do. To be going on with.

Doris A fiver?

Galbraith Verily.

Doris You're unspeakable. Unspeakable.

Galbraith Oh yes. I am a pariah, madam. I freely admit it. (*He prances about flapping his arms*)

Doris Stop it! Please stop it!

Galbraith (*declaiming loudly and gesticulating*) Woe unto them that call evil good and good evil; and put darkness for light and light for darkness. Woe unto them that are wise in their own eyes, and prudent in their own sight! Woe unto them who would cleanse their pimples with long combinations. Woe unto them——

Doris (*once more delving into her purse*) Here . . . here. It's all I have. (*She takes out two pound notes*) Take it. Take it and please go.

Galbraith (*taking the money*) Sufficient unto the day. I am not a greedy man. (*He prances up to his notice and takes it in one hand lifting it aloft*) Let us go up against Judah and vex it! Be of good heart, madam. Your alms will be well spent.

Doris On drink?

Galbraith And such like sustenance. A man must escape from time to time. Two pounds will hardly buy oblivion. But rest assured, madam, none of this (*waving the notes*) will be squandered on administrative costs.

Doris No, it will be wasted and perhaps somebody, somewhere could die for it.

Galbraith Ah. (*Thinking for a moment*) Well, it's all relative, madam. It's all relative. There are so many of us, you see. And we are everywhere. It all boils down to Sodom and Gomorrah when you come to think of it. And the people shall be oppressed every one by another. For ye have eaten up the vineyard and the spoil of the poor is in your house. It's in the book, madam. It's all in the book. I know. I've read it. Peace be with you.

Galbraith blesses her with his banner and exits L

The doorbell tinkles after him. Doris watches him go for a moment, her face troubled. She is near to tears

Doris exits L. *The doorbell tinkles, the door slams, and we hear it being locked*

Hilda enters DR

Hilda Doris?

Doris enters L, *still in a daze*

I think Brenda is back in the toilet. It really is too bad. What were you doing?

Doris What?

Hilda I said what were you doing?

Doris Locking up.

Hilda But it's not time. We stay open to five, you know that.

Doris I didn't want him back.

Hilda Who?

Doris Mr Galbraith.

Hilda (*indifferently*) Oh him. (*Going to the till*) Who's been fiddling with this? Mrs Pike, I suppose. She's far too old for this sort of thing.

Doris He makes me uneasy. I cannot cope with biblical quotations. They have an uneasy truth.

Hilda Biblical claptrap. The man's a crook. Did he ask you for money?

Doris Yes.

Hilda How much?

Doris Five pounds.

Hilda You didn't give him five pounds?

Doris I gave him two. It was all I had in my purse.

Hilda (*shaking her head*) Foolish.

Doris Well I got confused. (*Turning; quite fiercely*) And we created him, Hilda. The same as we created the others. (*To herself*) For you have eaten up the vineyard and the spoil of the poor is in your houses. That's true, you see. That's true.

Hilda It's senseless if you ask me. (*Going down to the staff entrance and looking out*) We really must get Brenda out of the toilet.

Doris We created Brenda too. And our eyes are closed, because we don't want to see.

Hilda For goodness' sake, Doris, pull yourself together. Galbraith's a crook. He goes round all the charity shops preying on people like you, and Brenda's a boozer. Nobody created them except themselves. (*Bellowing*) Have you finished in the toilet, Brenda? You don't own it you know.

Brenda (*hysterically; off*) Keep away! This is for ladies only.

Hilda One of these days I shall brain that woman.

Doris We pretend they don't exist, and they do. We created them, all of them. Everyone loveth gifts and followeth after rewards.

Hilda Are you drunk, Doris?

Doris I don't think so. It was just something that he said. And I think he was right.

Brenda (*shrieking; off*) There's a man in here, with yellow spats.

Hilda Oh Great God!

Doris Perhaps I should join the Salvation Army.

Brenda Help Help!

Doris collects her coat and shopping bag

Hilda (*furiously*) Shut up! (*To Doris*) Where are you going?

Doris Home. I don't think we can feed the world. I don't think we really want to. It's all so useless. So I might as well go home.

Hilda And leave Brenda in the lavatory?

Doris She'll be out in a minute, she never stays long with the man in yellow spats.

Hilda Supposing we all went home. Supposing we all went home and buried our heads. Would that be the answer?

Doris I don't know. I don't know.

Hilda Well I do and I know this. We may not be able to feed all the world, as you put it, but we can try to feed some of it. This is our purpose here. Oh I know you think we are in some way responsible for people like Galbraith and Brenda. Perhaps we are, perhaps charity does begin at home, here on our own doorstep. But I do know this: Galbraith and Brenda generally have enough to eat, they are not dying of starvation. The people we are trying to help have nothing. (*With fierce conviction*) Absolutely nothing. (*After a pause; in a slightly altered tone*) So if you want to go home, Doris, go. I shan't stop you. Go home. Escape. Put it out of your mind. There's plenty of palliatives, plenty of excuses. It's not too difficult to cover guilt by laughing at middle-aged women doing good works. But the guilt remains. (*After a pause; quietly*) They have eyes and see not. I bet Galbraith used that quotation. He generally does. It's part of his . repertoire.

Doris (*a little shaken*) You care ... I never ... I mean, you really care. You really care.

They look at each other for a long moment

Hilda (*practical again*) I care about that damned woman messing up my toilet. (*She moves to the staff entrance*) Come on, Brenda. Brenda. Doris is going. You can't stay there all night. Brenda!

Brenda emerges DR and flourishes past Hilda

Brenda There is no need to bellow at me like a Sergeant Major. I was only powdering my nose.

Hilda (*attempting some humour*) And what about the gentleman in the yellow spats?

Brenda (*raising her eyebrows*) I beg your pardon?

Hilda Oh, nowt. Nowt.

Hilda starts tidying up. Brenda gets her coat

Brenda Has anybody seen my shopping bag? It contains, amongst other things, one packet of fish fingers.

Doris (*retrieving Brenda's bag*) Here it is. (*She gives Brenda the bag and moves across to Hilda*) Are you coming?

Hilda No. There's a bit to do yet, and I'll have to cash up.

Doris Oh. (*She hesitates*) Well, perhaps I could ... er ...

Brenda (*plaintively*) I want to go home. I want to go home and lock the door. Keep out the men. You understand, Doris. You do understand?

Doris Of course I understand. I'll give you a lift in the car. I generally do.

Brenda Yes, yes. You're so good to me, Doris. So understanding. (*Looking forlorn and rather crumpled*) Life can be troublesome for the single woman.

Doris turns to Brenda, hesitates and turns back to Hilda

Hilda Go on, Doris. I can manage. (*A little sternly; to Brenda*) I always have and I always will.

Brenda Yes, but then you're the managing type, Hilda. (*She smiles, having made her point; once more sensing drama*) Oh God! I just hope I shan't be raped between here and the car park.

Brenda stalks out L. *The doorbell tinkles*

Hilda (*calling after her*) I shouldn't think it likely, it's barely a hundred yards.

Doris I'd better go.

Hilda (*laughing*) Yes.

Doris She gets excited, you see.

Hilda I had noticed. (*She goes on with her tidying up*)

Doris So I had better go. (*She puts her coat on and goes to the door* L) Hilda?

Hilda Yes.

Doris It is important? I mean, what we are doing. It is important, for us—if nobody else?

Hilda Of course it's important. I've told you.

Doris I know, I know. And I expect you're right. And about us: middle-aged women doing good works, playing at shopkeeping. Bit of a joke, really. Bit of a joke.

Hilda I don't suppose the people in the Third World are laughing too much. And those who find us funny now, might thank God for what we did in years to come.

Doris I hope so. I do hope so. Because you see I don't——

Hilda You'd best go, Doris. There's two pubs and an off-licence between here and the car park. Now that's temptation.

Doris Oh Lord, yes! Poor Brenda. You won't, I mean you——

Hilda She's a damned nuisance. But I suppose she's a cross I'll have to bear, along with Mr Galbraith.
Doris Sodom and Gomorrah.
Hilda What?
Doris Oh. (*She laughs*) Nothing. Well, I'd better pop along, you never know.
Hilda (*smiling*) You never know. Tarrar.
Doris Bye.

She exits L and re-enters a second later

Oh, I daresay I'll see you here next week.
Hilda Thanks, Doris. I thought you would.
Doris Yes ... yes. (*Waving*) Bye then.

Doris exits L. The doorbell tinkles. Hilda follows her out and locks the door. She returns and stands looking about her for a moment. She notices the empty bottle cast off by Brenda, picks it up, drops it in the bin and goes to the till. It works for Hilda. Everything works for Hilda

CURTAIN

FURNITURE AND PROPERTY LIST

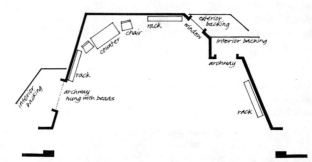

On stage: Trestle table covered with chenille cloth. *On it:* electric till (practical), various knick-knacks. *Behind it:* **Doris**'s shopping bag. **Brenda**'s shopping bag containing shopping and a half bottle of gin, waste bin

Shelves. *On them:* old toys, boxes of games etc.

2 bentwood chairs. *Against them:* tennis raquets, croquet mallets, umbrella etc.

Racks or tables containing old clothes on hangers and one empty hanger

Large cardboard boxes full of old clothes including a dress, pair of gent's patent leather shoes

Doris's coat

Mrs Pike's coat

Brenda's coat

Off stage: Plastic carrier bag **(Hilda)**

Cup and saucer **(Doris)**

Cup of tea **(Doris)**

Pair of gent's long combinations **(Mrs Pike)**

Notice which reads: MOAB SHALL HOWL OVER NEBO **(Galbraith)**

Cup of tea **(Doris)**

Personal: **Doris:** purse containing two £1 notes

EFFECTS PLOT

LIGHTING PLOT

Practical fittings required: electric till with flashing lights
Interior. The same scene throughout

To open: General interior lighting with pale sunlight through
dusty window

Cue 1   Till pings, zips etc.   (Page 14)
           Lights on till flash

MADE AND PRINTED IN GREAT BRITAIN BY
LATIMER TREND & COMPANY LTD PLYMOUTH

MADE IN ENGLAND